I Like Pie

by Kyle Schmeck

Illustrated by Gary Undercuffler

1

To my parents, Buddy and Jackie Lou,
who taught me to read with passion, write with creativity and leisurely
enjoy a delicious piece of homemade Rhubarb pie.

God bless you, Mother, and rest in peace.
I'm sorry you never saw the final result.

Acknowledgements

Thanks to my friends who helped me complete this book:

Brandi Chawaga for reading my first draft to Liam and Avery
Tammy Tarloski for her insight and assistance
Rich Nave for his counsel and connections
Julie Guarna for her artistic ideas and leading me to Gary U
Gary Undercuffler for his beautifully designed sketches

Special thanks to Ruth Cole for accidentally giving me inspiration on a
routine car ride to work several years ago

And finally to Kalyn Roberts for her on-going personal interest, guidance
and support

I like pie.

Why Daddy, why do you like pie?

I like pie. Just because ... that's why.

Daddy, what kind of pie would you like to buy?

I like Blueberry pie.
Blueberry pie is what I'd buy.

Daddy, I like apple pie.
I would climb high for apple pie.

6

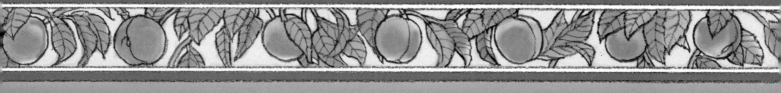

Darling, do you like Peach pie?

I like Peach pie. I like Peach on the beach under a big blue sky.

Would you try Lemon pie?

I like Lemon pie. It's wiggly and yummy like jelly on rye.

How about Cherry pie?

I like Cherry pie. It makes me so happy
I could fly.

Is Pumpkin a pie you would try?

I like Pumpkin pie. After turkey dinner
it's the best pie to try.

Do you like Pecan pie?

I like Pecan pie. Mommy bakes it so pretty it catches my eye.

Would you buy a Key Lime pie?

I like Key Lime pie. It reminds me of summer, and I don't know why.

Do you like Shoo Fly pie?

No Daddy, no. Please no flies on my pie.

How about a Mudpie?

You're silly, Daddy. Eating mudpies makes me cry.

Do you know the name of my favorite pie?

No Daddy, what is your favorite pie?

It's you, my darling, my Sweetie Pie!

24

Made in the USA
Columbia, SC
17 February 2020